The Book of Night & Waking

The Book of Night & Waking
© Clif Mason / Cathexis Northwest Press

No part of this book may be reproduced without written permission of the
publisher or author, except in reviews and articles.

First Printing: 2020

Paperback ISBN: 978-1-7342842-6-3

Cover Art, Design & Editing by C. M. Tollefson

Cathexis Northwest Press

cathexisnorthwestpress.com

The Book of Night & Waking

by Clif Mason

Cathexis Northwest Press

Proem

We lived in a time of war,

                                           in which every door
       was blackened with loss
             & every street was electric
                                           with angers
             & resentments.
Every home seethed
             with unanswerable questions.
      & at least one that wanted an answer.
What's to keep us from leaving
                               right now
          & walking to Antarctica?

You put down the cloth
                            on which you were sewing
       a phantasmagoria of beads,
                            smiled & said,
        Oh, maybe a few hundred of miles
                 of cold ocean.
     I hear it doesn't take kindly to foot traffic.
                                     No,
           we must each find our own way
           to face down the darkness.
                This is mine.

You lifted the round-framed cloth,
                                  painstakingly adorned,
      hour after dreaming,
                  patient hour,
    with a splendor & dazzle

                                                        of beads.
Sunlight struck,
                    seized,
                                    & defined each color,
            shape,
            & texture.

I could say nothing.

Go ahead,
            walk this long walk,
                                    you said at last,
                            filling the air
        with the words
                    of which I'd been incapable.
I'll give you, what,
                a year?
                                Then I'll take a plane
                    & wait for you
                            at the Amundsen-Scott Station.

Why don't you sail?
        Shackleton's ship looked all wild
                                            & weird
                in the black-&-white photographs—
        remember —
                    all frost-rimed,
                                        its rigging hung
                        with icicles,
                as if festooned
                        for some winter solstice party.

They don't even make ships like that anymore.
It's a plane or nothing for me.

We swam all night
                      in the moon's golden lake
    until, at dawn,
             we read from the book
                           of waking,
      every page luminous
                & transparent. Green light on
morning's tongue,
                        a song sung
      even in the shadows.
Trees galloped,
        a hundred horses in the wind.
Flowers lifted their heads,
                a thousand blackbirds
      winging from the earth.

I didn't know
        the length of my journey
       didn't know if I'd end the same person
              I'd begun.
But I trusted
       the red compass of my blood,
    & without another moment's worry
                    or hesitation,
      I set out,
      carrying my satchel of words
              & new stars.

For Laurie

And that love is a kelson of the creation . . .
Walt Whitman

Acknowledgments

I am grateful to the editors of these magazines,
in whose pages versions of sections of this poem appeared:

Evergreen Review: Section 13
(as "Lunar Dispossession")

Filling the Empty Room: Section 3
(as "The Human Communion of Salt")

The Lyric: The formal lines interpolated in sections 9 and 18
(as "Against Caution" and "Don Giovanni's Night Music,"
respectively)

Abiding gratitude to:
C. M. Tollefson of *Cathexis Northwest Press*
and to John Sibley Williams.

Special thanks also to Marjorie Saiser and Joseph Fasano.

Contents

The Book of Night & Waking: 19

Notes: 63

1.

As apples dreamed on the cemetery earth,

                                      the owl

        read the book of night—
    kenned its braille
        as easily as someone reads

                                  these lines—

            & blue winds
    ghosted around the trees.

Talons gripped the rabbit,
              & blood burned

                            in my body
                like a star.

Daybreak spoke
    her first green vowels

              & on all sides

                            birdsong
        lifted something resembling

                          happiness
    from the grass blades

            to the highest boughs.

Sun struck
        & severed the clouds,

                    like a butchered cow,
    & bright blood sprayed

            from east to west.

Sun emerged

        & stunned
                every animate & inanimate thing,
     struck fire,
liquid, breathing flame—
                  from rocks & pebbles,
        from cliff faces & stone outcroppings,
            from dust itself.

Molten rivers laid claim
                to whatever was comforted
     or contorted
by my name—
                both the elements known
        & those that would never be known.

To my surprise, the sun didn't vaporize
                  my face
     or the consonants of my speech
or the craftiness of my fingers.
Instead, she chose to preserve them—
     like one of Herculaneum's intricate mosaics,
            only alive.

2.

Hold this bead tight in your grasp,
you'd said,
taking it from a red silk pouch
& placing it in my hand.
Say my name & I will be with you,
wherever you are on this earth.

She'd made the bead:
It was half as big as my thumb
& was black.
Yet it had an endless array
of sparks within,
like the night sky.

I clasped the bead & you appeared.
A star began to sing on my tongue,
& if we waited
to learn the words,
the song would be finished.
Explosions on another continent
peeled skin from our flesh
& glass slivers pierced our cheeks.
Pain took apart everything,
even poetry.

Neither mountains nor stars
were permanent,
just imponderably
slow,
in their infidelity.

The white water of longing
                                      abraded our skin.
When I stepped into your green chapel,
                      I felt shockwave & heat,
    as if lightning had struck
        ten steps off,
                                ripping the air apart,
    stripping it of all but ozone.
Stars were tattooed on night's jet skin,
                        & the moon shriveled
        like a leaf.

3.

The stillness of silk & silt.
To what silence can I cling
    that is salient
        in the night?
Do I know the simple objects
     of my daily walk,
  of my journey through trees
       & elusive stars?
How do I measure the vagaries
      & variance
   of the real & unreal?

Always the sound of water,
      the purl & purr
        of its flowing,
   its carving & reaching.
I heard it because it sought me out,
       searched for the echo
   in my flesh,
  the movement in my blood.
I heard it because it entered
      & streamed through us,
  because it lit up my brain
     & lisped & lapped
   at every hidden cove & shore,
   at the long, unknown beaches within.

Currents carried me to depths
        yet unplumbed,

so I might know more
      than fever dream or drama,
    pearl or peril.
Waves washed away debts & forgetfulness,
       doubts & regrets.
They removed the deaths & dearths
     in which I conspired.
When I was cleansed once more,
      what acts would I own
  on the daybreak streets—
      with the sound of water
  in my ears,
     & in my mind the ceaseless,
  unbroken cheer & chant
    of the water vespers?

4.

The day the war started,
                the river flowed past
                              in its calibrated banks.
The birds were noisy
                & then they were quiet.
Before,
        death had been a matter of bodies giving out
                              over time
                or failing of an instant,
      of accidents,
               or of sudden hatreds & blind blows.
Now no death was unprecedented.
No death was even unusual.
Death had become life's most common datum,
                              ordinary as greed
          or the desire for revenge.

No one claimed to want the war,
                      & yet everyone had a hand in it.
The killing & the dying
            became the rhythm of the day.
Refugees streamed out of the hills
                & forests & down the dusty roads.
They came all day
        & all night for weeks,
                            until there were millions
            in the camps.
There was no firewood & little food—
                only what people carried.

Cholera & dysentery
                     spread like rumors through the tents.

After a few weeks,
                     bands of men began to attack families.
They stole food & beat the men
                     & held them at knifepoint
      as they raped their wives
                                & daughters
                 & mothers & sisters.
Afterwards they cut everyone's throats,
                            even the children's,
           even the infants'.
People saw their days darken,
                   & they knew what men did in the dark.

Husbands & wives still married,
                            children still found their way
           into this world.
A few people wrote books,
                         & a few more read them.
Battles did not end the war,
                         but led only to other battles.
More & more land
               was given over to graveyards.
The moon still rose,
                         the stars still appeared.
The sun still marched without mercy
                         across the sky's battlefield.
The living didn't notice
                   & the dead didn't care.

The river flowed by,

      the birds flew away—
           leaving stray feathers
  for poets & vagabonds to find.
The war went on.
Life went on—
     & life had always been war.
Everyone said so.
 It would still be war
     when the last of the midnight stars
   blinked out.
No one doubted it,
    not even children.
This was the way things were,
       & the way things were
  was the way things would always be,
      forever & ever,
   without end.
Only the dead stars believed in peace.

5.

I held the jet bead, & you were with me.
Your mouth was full of blue flowers,
                my hands were cupped with rain.

We have this brief time, you said.

Walk with me, I said,
        between the midwife's hands
    & summary execution,
      between first stars & last dreams.

Your arms were rivers
        burning with reflected stars,
    mine the aurora
        reaching out in banners of silk
                & milk
          streaming toward you
    in coral-flaming heraldry,
        carmine & green & golden.

Tell me a story,
    you said,
        of broken bodies & forsaken delights.

Walk with me, I said,
        between the pang & the pain,
  between the sea's sultry sighs & shrieks
      & the sun's forbidden gleams & glamor.

Your mouth was a new star

     spilling silver
           into ebony night,
  filling it with a luster
      of frost & opal & pearl.
My eyes were dark unseen moons.

What can we do when falling stars
         streak into the sea?

Walk with me & we'll learn the fever
         impelling us from this street
  to as far away as Antarctica
     & to the farthest star's incendiary heart.

6.

There was a horizon
                beyond any horizon,
                              a depth
      beneath all depth.

Questions questioned questions,
                        & answers hid
          in plain sight.

I didn't mind.
I knew every place
                was the center
                        of every other place.

No matter what happened,
                I was covered.

7.

In the humid air of misty midnight,
                              I walked in disbelief
    through the dispossessed streets
            of a small town.
Clouds lowered,
                        dense as the oozy mud
    of a river bottom,
        & throughout their massive,
                              confused bulk,
        they were infused with flame—
    no rusty ferrous sheen,
no blush or flush,
                but a blood-red voracious fire.

Let me repeat,
        this was no mellow glow,
                as of half-smothered embers,
    but a deep ruddled burn,
        a combusting flash
                            & shock-blast
            of black smoke
  & dark forest inferno—
                    a fulmination
    of scarlet-raging cumulonimbus.
I felt scorched,
        blistered,
                cremated mid-step.

Did the townspeople writhe, too,
                                              as they dreamed
        in their sweat-drenched sheets,
                in sympathy with my sudden pain?
Walking, I felt a baleful heat
                          rolling out of that burning sky.
        Neither sinless
                      nor particularly sinful,
          I shuddered at the flaming angel passing by.

8.

Why do I walk here,
        trudge through a land
                cracked
           & ravined
    as a fractured skull?
Why do I set one canvas-shod foot
              in front of the other—
        my own private death march—
    forsaken & fugitive,
            dream-curdled & futile?
The answer was the single
        incandescent word:
                Antarctica.
Just to say it was to feel the burn
              of subzero air
        on my face.

The land was so cold,
            snow almost never fell.
The continent, once wed to India,
        Australia, & South America,
    was covered by two miles of ice.
Its tallest mountain rose three miles.
The South Pole itself
        was ten thousand feet high.
There was no mining,
      so the land was arsenic-
              & zinc-free,
      nitrous oxide-free,
    hydrogen sulfide-free.

It was a land without government.
The emperor penguins & orcas
                              did not wage war.
Nor did the blue whales & colossal squids.
Even humans accepted it as a Zone of Peace.
No limbs were severed there,
                              no bodies maimed.
No blood was blown out of hearts,
                    no thoughts out of brains.

In the land of infinite whiteness,
                              of crisp starkness,
     I sought the correcting of my vision,
                              the clarity of ice
          in my blood & marrow.
& I sought love,
                    for I knew my beloved
                              would be waiting
                    at long journey's end,
          with encircling arms
                    & a welcoming kiss.

For love.
I drank from my water bottle,
                              &, sweating,
                    set one determined foot
          before the other.
                              For love.

9.

In my hand a bead,
     & in that bead
        the blackness of space opened.
When the city was indentured to time & fear,
        we were freakish
    as feldspar,
   as Greek spearmint—
        a smell like green smoke,
   fearless & eerie in the mouth,
    & lingering,

      lingering.

Surrounded by those endless cautious men,
   those too cautious women—who sprang up like
bamboo shoots, spurting skywards, not inches
   but feet each day, impaling hope on spikes.

You wanted boundless pastures
         of will & gold.
I wanted submarine shores
       of marl & rose.
Your tongue was a chalice.
Your shoulder,
   bare star,
        became barren harrow of bone,
  became errant morning,
       brash rain

Surrounded by those cautious souls who spoke
   of life's cheer as desert, I yearned for you,

who briskly carried me past risk, who broke
*   the hinges from the doors, led me to the new.*

You wanted the blind flame
                      of the total solar eclipse.
I wanted the music of mirrors
                        & magnesium.
We flamed,
        acetylene,
                      in an ice-locked lake,
    melted it with molten muscle
                      & blood.
We galloped on horses strong & fleet
                      across fields
        flat as tambourines.

To know you, love, my Aladdin's spellcraft lamp,
    from whom I summoned the genie of courage,
was to feel impressed on face the bright-edged stamp
    of joy, to hear the soul's reply to age.

You opened your eyes
                      & I felt star-burn.
Afternoon grew obsidian walls
                      & chill held the trees
        in amorous arms.
We turned to the room of heartbeat
                      & jewel.
Bedposts kindled.
We kissed.

Oh, love, take me to that far country where
    caution becomes daring & we fly through air.

10.

& then the women were gone.
A plowshare dredged a girl's groin,
                                          a red star
                        fell on her windpipe.
Her brain smoked like liquid nitrogen,
            & she struggled in a delirium of ghosts
                                  & forgotten time
                        to rise.
Her eyes were meteors
                        burning up in the night sky.
She sutured her own mouth shut
                        with black thread
        & wasted,
                        waned like the bulimic moon.
The old woman said she still saw her in Juárez,
                                a single star
                floating in infinite blackness.

Inside the ant's cathedral,
                night exhaled a rose
                          of stars & iron,
        of helium & salt.
There was no forgiveness.
Everyone was nailed to the stone
                        of time's indifference.
Rapists' fingerprints grew gray spiders
                            & knife blades.
Their foreheads dripped sweat
                    & steel springs,
        lizards & stunted trees.

Morning's light was thin
                & burnt out,
                              with an undreamt of pallor.
Air quivered with heat.
It shrank the skins of tarantulas
                & made the cactus thorns brittle,
        dryly brutal,
    complicit in the wind-blown murders
                      of moths & small birds.
People's shadows bled scorpion tails,
                              hawk beaks,
            & rattlesnake scales.

The city was no longer a city
                      but a morgue.
Death was the green bird
                flying from house to house
    & in each home a mother died,
                      or a daughter died.
It sang & a hundred women
                fell dead at once.
It sang
        & the cemeteries sprang up.
It sang & the living wept inconsolably
                & smeared ashes on their faces.

The green bird flew in & out of houses
                              & churches,
            stores & factories.
The bird flew faster
                & no one could catch it.
The women continued to fall.
They fell in the night & in the day.
The women continued to fall.

11.

In my grasp
                the bead that was night itself.
You kissed the black pearls of my eyes.
I touched gold moonlight on your neck.
We talked & our children were adopted,
                              born anew,
& fostered into our family—
                snuggling against us,
        blind as newborn otters.

We talked & night bled indigo,
                apricot,
                      blood rose—
        the colors of your paintings.
& when we were silent,
                my words were inked
                      on air's transparent page.

I touched starlight,
                pale as rain on your neck.
You took me in the moonbow of your arms.
I kissed the jade tiger-fire of your eyes.

12.

Down silicate dunes,
        across impossible dreams
            of black glass & red clay,
    the horsemen rode—
        seven, implacable,
                aloof,
            commanding.
Their horses' hooves,
        ringed in steel,
            rang clean on stone,
    sang of missed days
        & forlorn nights,
      of the broken chances
        that always spell a desolation of wants.
The night's hair was braided
        with weeping.
The day's winding cloth
            was woven of weeping.

Factories spilled their workers' preserved hearts,
    their pickled spirits,
        into the green maw of determined
      & interminable desire.
Smokestacks choked the sleek wind,
            wrapped their wire scarves
    round its slim neck
& squeezed until the air
        was still as desert rock,
    until storm sewers thrust up
        a torrent of dead dogs.

Weeping filled the air
                              with the cold taste of remorse.
Weeping filled the air
                              with the smoke of unseen fires.

The horsemen rode into a mountain village.
The air was thin
                              & the horses were breathing hard.
The men dismounted
                              & drank cups full of spiders
                & delicate webs
                      from the abandoned well.
Their horses slurped scorpions from a dry trough.
The men eyed the sun
                        hung at the meridian,
                              a desiccated bread crust,
            a rough quartz icon.
That morning only mourning doves sang,

                                        weeping.
That evening only bats & owls prayed,

                                          weeping.

Orphans trailed through the immolated streets.
Beggars collapsed into dust
                                  & rotted teeth.
All the houses were littered with dying mice.
The houseflies
                wriggled their eyelash-thin feet
                              in slow but resolute death.
Yet empty clothes still got up
                                  & went to work,
        & empty clothes
                    still put their checks in the bank.

Weeping filled the plates
       with coal grit & ash.
Weeping filled the pantry
       with steel filings & sand.

The horsemen could not make their horses stand up.
They sent their last bullets
         through the windows
    of the horses' skulls,
  watched them bleed
         ball bearings
       & toothless gear wheels
   & miles of rust.
There was no shade
      so the horsemen collapsed
        against a compound's fence,
   topped with razor wire.
As sun flamed to earth,
       they gagged on their tongues.
Nothing was heard for a long time,
        not even weeping.
Nothing was heard for a long time,
        not even weeping.

13.

The whole town fell asleep
                         & did not waken for days
     & when the people awoke,
          they all went around asking each other
                   about their dreams.

Do you remember?
Her face was a bowl of lemons.
Where are the black dogs?
There were hundreds of black dogs.
& the whole sky turned to numbers.
Each star was a maze of equations.
Did you see the trees become green bears
               & fish salmon from the rivers?
For a whole day,
      the rain flew up
               in torrents from the earth.
        & afterwards,
lakes floated darkly above new deserts.

But the more they learned,
                     the less they knew,
       & they became sullen & confused.
They vowed never to sleep again.
& so far they haven't.

They are guarded, nervous,
             & quick to suspect their neighbors.
All night they walk in circles on their hands
                    so as not to doze off.
All day they cut nicks on their arms & legs.

It isn't sleep they fear but dreams.
They have made dreaming illegal
                                    & speaking of dreams
              & writing them down
          & making songs of them
                                        & filming them
               & making ballets & plays.
They no longer touch each other
                                    in tenderness or desire.
Their tongues grow used to silence,
                  their eyes to permanent vigilance.
They do not know how long they can last.
They do not realize
                   they were awake when they dreamed,
      & are now asleep.
I'm waiting for the first to waken.

14.

Walking up a steep path,
       I heard these words:
  Climb from the jaguar's forest
        to the Inca's house.
Walk through the trapezoidal door
    into time
       & slavery
         & execution.
& as you work in the midnight graves
        of the silver mines,
     hold fast to your desire to drink,
  like the condor,
     the air between mountain peaks,
    to walk sure-footed as a llama
        up the rocks.

Desire the green fire
      of mountain air in your lungs,
      desire the truth
  like an obsidian blade in your chest.
The mines have—
    & will always have—
         new masters.
Only words can smash your manacles.
Only words can make you masterless.

Take this path all the way
       to Tierra del Fuego,
Clouds show the way.
Kind words are your passport,
      yet no one trusts them,

so be prepared to steal across borders.
You may never return—
but you knew that when you started.

15.

The midnight bead brought my love to me.
We talked until she fell asleep,
                        her head on the moon's hand.
My breath became braided in her hair
        & my eyes stroked her cheeks & neck.
As my fingers traced her arm's warm cinnamon,
                      I kissed the line on her throat
        between shadow & light,
    kissed her temples,
                      where larks hid themselves,
        kissed her forehead,
            where dreams played out,
                            disembodied
                    as the light at the ruby's heart.
Singing her name,
                syllables soft as eyelashes on cheeks,
    I lay down beside her to sleep,
        my head on the moon's other hand.

16.

Rain hauled up the tall mainsails
                                        of the forest
         & forced grass' soft follicles.
Dead comrades lay still
                        under the canopies.
The great Chilean poet
              spoke what they could not.
In the wet season
      the moon drank until its belly bulged,
               until it became sodden
           & denuded of desire.
The rising sun scuttled a fleet of clouds.
He dived deep into the sea
                & leaped up again in flames.

Beneath the planet's green skin,
      its fertile black shell,
            & beneath the mountains,
        great flat slabs & porous shelves,
needle spikes & blunt bluffs & boulders—
          all chanted a single continuous tone,
     deeper than any gong or bell.
In the earth, the dead heard it,
      & they opened their cold bony mouths
                to intone it, too.
From the old stones,
     he learned to sing in the key of the dead,
         that he might solace the living.

17.

I wore out a pair of shoes
                before I reached the rock-strewn shore
    of southern Argentina
      & stood, at the very end of day,
                  like Balboa gazing rapt
        at the vast expanse of the Pacific—
yes, I stared straight across the Strait of Magellan
    at the distant broken-boned islands
              of Tierra del Fuego.

I faced serious water for the first time.
The ocean was far more imposing
                & imperial
      in its relentlessness
          than the lakes I had swum,
    the innumerable creeks I had splashed across,
      or the rivers I had forded.
There, on the last rocky outpost
              of the landmass,
    the sea winds strove to topple me
        from my perch into the waves,
      as they smashed against the continent
                & sprayed up,
      in splendid,
               exquisite futility
    toward the millions of emerging stars.

An orca breached & swam toward me.
I felt summoned,
          commanded to walk out
        onto the wide white wake of the moon.

My blood flamed in answer,
                        & even if it were to my death,
       I had to obey.
I stepped off the boulder,
                        ready for the drop,
    the frozen submersion.
Instead, I stepped onto the orca's back.
He turned
           & churned through the choppy water,
                      & I strove to stay upright.

We were soon in deepest ocean.
Water spray sheathed my clothes & hair in ice.
Only some pure fire within
                              kept me from freezing.
The orca swam faster than a speedboat,
                      more steadily than a ship.
It never tired,
            though I thought I would expire
      from exhaustion.

Just when I knew I could no longer stand
                        & I began the slow,
        inexorable fall
    into turbulent black water,
                    we arrived,
                     &, impelled by our motion,
    I flew onto the vast snow-&-ice-covered land.
My blood blazed
           & I struggled to my feet.
I stood & looked toward the sea,
                      but the orca was gone.

I turned & began to trek—
       in a trance—
              to the interior,
    over ice two miles thick.
I don't know how many days it was
          before I arrived at the Station,
   but when I did, there she was,
             my artist wife,
     loyal beyond my lunacy.

& there,
     in the land where the air was so cold
         it didn't rain
    & almost never snowed,
  where most of the world's fresh water
           lay locked in a block
        as big as a country,
    there love set aflame the body
       that had dwelled in peril
          & nearly perished.
I felt hot as the summer day
           I'd started my long walk.
& I felt peace,
      real peace.

18.

A song's lament
                      surprised like coconut milk
                                        on your lips.
Let me drink it again.
I hung the moon,
            a feather,
                      in your hair,
                          & we were rose quartz
              & moonstone.
Hands searched
                & we touched
                          in a silver landscape
                      of memory & requital.

Time, the pickpocket prince, will steal us old
        Give me a horse with wings, a shooting star.
Let's take this leaden hour & make it gold
        We ride this night to Venus. Is it far?

Give me that guitar,
                lush as bougainvillea,
                        weeping arterial light into day.
The song wreathed us like smoke,
                            slid like smoke between.
I touched it on your shoulders
                      & in the midnight roses of your hair.
The song spiraled down long legs,
                          spilled down arms.

Give me a horse with wings, a shooting star
        The moon cuts deep into its midnight groove

We ride this night to Venus. Is it far?
    Even the sweetest times we can improve.

We spoke
        & dark nebulae floated between us,
                a swirling syllable dance.
Lips found lips
        & words became kisses,
    flaming strings of prominences,
                solar winds.
Touch became eloquent speech.
The song poured from me into you
                & back into me.

The moon cuts deep into its midnight groove
    We blaze through ice, for all the world to see
that even the sweetest times we can improve.
    We burn forever, escape mortality.

We let the guitarist's gracile fingers
                trill staccato fire
        up spines.
Skin flushed with song,
                flesh sang with beat & blood.
We let that guitar play through me,
                through you,
        through endless night & waking.

We blaze through ice, for all the world to see
    Oh, let me move you now, & deeply move,
We burn forever, escape mortality.
    I will not live by halves, nor will I love

Sidereal furnaces consumed planets
                           & moons
            & desire's corona burned
                                 beyond flame,
               until we reached the final,
      infinite, tender collapse within,
                    to ineffable density,
             a gravity so great
          nothing but these words could escape.

Notes:

The Whitman epigraph is from "Song of Myself."

The Chilean poet referenced in section 16 is Pablo Neruda. The allusion is to section XII of "The Heights of Macchu Picchu," specifically the line, "I come to speak through your dead mouth" (translation by Mariela Griffor).

Also Available
from
Cathexis Northwest Press:

<u>Something To Cry About</u>
by Robert Krantz

<u>Suburban Hermeneutics</u>
by Ian Cappelli

<u>God's Love Is Very Busy</u>
by David Seung

<u>that one time we were almost people</u>
by Christian Czaniecki

<u>Fever Dream/Take Heart</u>
by Valyntina Grenier

Cathexis Northwest Press

www.ingramcontent.com/pod-product-compliance
Lightning Source LLC
Chambersburg PA
CBHW021132080526
44587CB00012B/1251